BREXIT: A NEGOTIATION UPDATE

HEARING

BEFORE THE

SUBCOMMITTEE ON EUROPE, EURASIA, AND EMERGING THREATS

OF THE

COMMITTEE ON FOREIGN AFFAIRS
HOUSE OF REPRESENTATIVES

ONE HUNDRED FIFTEENTH CONGRESS

FIRST SESSION

DECEMBER 6, 2017

Serial No. 115–100

Printed for the use of the Committee on Foreign Affairs

Available via the World Wide Web: http://www.foreignaffairs.house.gov/ or
http://www.gpo.gov/fdsys/

U.S. GOVERNMENT PUBLISHING OFFICE

27–757PDF   WASHINGTON : 2018

For sale by the Superintendent of Documents, U.S. Government Publishing Office
Internet: bookstore.gpo.gov   Phone: toll free (866) 512–1800; DC area (202) 512–1800
Fax: (202) 512–2104   Mail: Stop IDCC, Washington, DC 20402–0001

COMMITTEE ON FOREIGN AFFAIRS

EDWARD R. ROYCE, California, *Chairman*

CHRISTOPHER H. SMITH, New Jersey
ILEANA ROS-LEHTINEN, Florida
DANA ROHRABACHER, California
STEVE CHABOT, Ohio
JOE WILSON, South Carolina
MICHAEL T. McCAUL, Texas
TED POE, Texas
DARRELL E. ISSA, California
TOM MARINO, Pennsylvania
MO BROOKS, Alabama
PAUL COOK, California
SCOTT PERRY, Pennsylvania
RON DeSANTIS, Florida
MARK MEADOWS, North Carolina
TED S. YOHO, Florida
ADAM KINZINGER, Illinois
LEE M. ZELDIN, New York
DANIEL M. DONOVAN, JR., New York
F. JAMES SENSENBRENNER, JR.,
  Wisconsin
ANN WAGNER, Missouri
BRIAN J. MAST, Florida
FRANCIS ROONEY, Florida
BRIAN K. FITZPATRICK, Pennsylvania
THOMAS A. GARRETT, JR., Virginia
JOHN R. CURTIS, Utah

ELIOT L. ENGEL, New York
BRAD SHERMAN, California
GREGORY W. MEEKS, New York
ALBIO SIRES, New Jersey
GERALD E. CONNOLLY, Virginia
THEODORE E. DEUTCH, Florida
KAREN BASS, California
WILLIAM R. KEATING, Massachusetts
DAVID N. CICILLINE, Rhode Island
AMI BERA, California
LOIS FRANKEL, Florida
TULSI GABBARD, Hawaii
JOAQUIN CASTRO, Texas
ROBIN L. KELLY, Illinois
BRENDAN F. BOYLE, Pennsylvania
DINA TITUS, Nevada
NORMA J. TORRES, California
BRADLEY SCOTT SCHNEIDER, Illinois
THOMAS R. SUOZZI, New York
ADRIANO ESPAILLAT, New York
TED LIEU, California

AMY PORTER, *Chief of Staff*   THOMAS SHEEHY, *Staff Director*

JASON STEINBAUM, *Democratic Staff Director*

SUBCOMMITTEE ON EUROPE, EURASIA, AND EMERGING THREATS

DANA ROHRABACHER, California, *Chairman*

JOE WILSON, South Carolina
TED POE, Texas
TOM MARINO, Pennsylvania
F. JAMES SENSENBRENNER, JR.,
  Wisconsin
FRANCIS ROONEY, Florida
BRIAN K. FITZPATRICK, Pennsylvania
JOHN R. CURTIS, Utah

GREGORY W. MEEKS, New York
BRAD SHERMAN, California
ALBIO SIRES, New Jersey
WILLIAM R. KEATING, Massachusetts
DAVID N. CICILLINE, Rhode Island
ROBIN L. KELLY, Illinois

CONTENTS

Page

WITNESSES

LETTERS, STATEMENTS, ETC., SUBMITTED FOR THE HEARING

APPENDIX

BREXIT: A NEGOTIATION UPDATE

WEDNESDAY, DECEMBER 6, 2017

HOUSE OF REPRESENTATIVES,
SUBCOMMITTEE ON EUROPE, EURASIA, AND EMERGING THREATS,
COMMITTEE ON FOREIGN AFFAIRS,
Washington, DC.

The subcommittee met, pursuant to notice, at 2:00 p.m., in room 2200 Rayburn House Office Building, Hon. Dana Rohrabacher (chairman of the subcommittee) presiding.

Mr. ROHRABACHER. I call to order this hearing of the Europe, Eurasia, and Emerging Threats Subcommittee.

The topic for this afternoon's hearing is the United Kingdom's exit from the European Union and to understand better where those negotiations currently stand.

The Brexit vote represents a self-determination of the British people. It reflects an inherent desire of people to control their own destiny rather than be under the domination of another country or another group of countries.

Around the world, populations are increasingly seeking to exercise their right of self-determination. When done peacefully through the ballot box, such as what happened in the United Kingdom and, I might add, in the United Kingdom as happened to Scotland, I believe the world would be a much better place if people were allowed to make that choice in that peaceful manner.

After 40 years of membership in the EU and its predecessor organizations, the British people voted last year by a clear margin to end that membership.

It has set the U.K. on a course which I guess would be on March— in March 2019 for exit. Between now and that date, a wide variety of issues remain to be resolved.

Many speculate that the major pieces of the transition must be set far ahead of that date in order to allow industry and business to adapt to the new rules.

Both sets of negotiation and the negotiating teams appear to be dedicated to approaching their task with good will. But the breadth and complexity of the challenges would be imposing on any group of people trying to find those type of solutions.

While I have great sympathy for those in Britain who want to return political power from Brussels to London and believe that the EU countries—there probably are other EU countries who want to follow their lead.

But whatever decision people make in terms of their own self-determination, clearly, Americans have friends on both sides of this issue and are inclined to support people who are longing for their freedom as—and representative government.

As my colleagues and I get into this discussion with the panelists, I especially want to talk about Ireland and learn what progress has been made to ensure there will be no hard border between the Republic of Ireland and Northern Ireland.

The return to a hard border, I fear, would be a needless blow to the peace process that has achieved so much in that part of the world over the last few decades.

The United States is, of course, not a party to the Brexit negotiations. But we do have a keen interest in what the outcome of those negotiations will come up with.

I hope to learn from our witnesses how the United States Congress can play a positive and constructive role as both sides work to establish a new relationship.

I also want to recognize that several members of the Irish Parliament are with us today and we welcome you. And let me just say this. I have a special place in my heart for Ireland.

I learned all about the real political facts of life from the greatest Irish American President, Ronald Reagan, who—with whom I spoke and met and worked with for 7½ years of my life in the White House. So it is a pleasure to have you here with us.

And let us also note—my staff didn't put this in my notes—but let us also note that the Irish were really beside the Americans, were the first ones to strike a blow for self-determination and we are happy that their British—their former British landlords now have learned a lesson and are now establishing early self-determination in Europe.

So welcome aboard. And thanks to our witnesses. And without objection, all the members will have 5 legislative days to submit any written questions for you.

I would appreciate if you would basically limit your testimony to 5 minutes each and then open up for the members to ask what questions they have and we could have a dialogue.

With that said, I recognize my ranking member, Mr. Meeks, and who we worked together very well and this shows you just how people can work together with various different points of view. I would say enough for my Irish parliamentarians over there.

Mr. MEEKS. Indeed. Thank you, Mr. Chairman. I want to thank you also for calling this timely conversation on the Brexit negotiations.

To be honest, I see the Brexit process as a lose-lose-lose situation. The UK, the EU, and the United States—in other words, the West, will take an economic and political hit.

Of course, there may be small pockets of economic winners joined by cultural elites who will benefit. The vote did reflect real grievances with the status quo.

America, meanwhile, is losing its closest ideological ally in the European Union and the influence that came with it in Great Britain.

Many remain to believe that Brexit negotiations will be simple— that the EU would succumb to the British demands and a global Britain will emerge, ready to strike trade deals and still be able to set rules and standards at home.

In the past weeks, though, reality is beginning to bite. More specifically, the Northern Island question—something my colleagues on both sides of the aisle care deeply about, is unresolved.

The Good Friday agreement, a delicate consensus that we helped foster, is at risk. The essential question for the Irish Government, and they have been—and they have the backing of the EU with their veto just as every member state does, and this is just one example of the similarly countless hurdles in the negotiations that must end in March 2019. That is, unless there is a transition period on extension as agreed upon.

The March 2019 deadline was imposed by the UK when it triggered Article 50, thereby starting the 2-year clock.

Other red lines were perhaps prematurely set early such as the refusal to entertain the customs union as an option, done without considering the economic consequences.

Must of the Prime Minister's government, including the Prime Minister herself, campaigned to remain. These questions are all related or complicated and the EU is negotiating from a unified position with a weak partner government. Not sure about what it wants.

In the realm of bilateral U.S.-U.K. trade, we learned in our February hearing that there is not much to gain nor is it clear when we could even start negotiating, given the practical constraints.

The potential gains are either not there, already exhausted, or protected. In reality, the U.K. would be coming to American negotiators looking for a deal, any deal. In our negotiations, we look to extract the best deal for America.

So what does this mean for the special relationship? Reckless hateful tweets from our Presidential—from our President aside, and with the help of delicious British imports we will carry on.

Our histories and our political ties are stronger than that. We will continue to work closely with the U.K. and NATO and encourage the U.K. to continue to support sanctions in the Kremlin.

In the Brexit negotiations, as highlighted by Prime Minister May in Philadelphia, our close relationship with a strong EU is in both America's and the U.K.'s interest.

In that spirit, I hope the U.K. and the EU remain very close partners that we, the United States, can count on and cooperate with.

I encourage both sides to avoid the cliff edge no-deal scenario. Come back to reality and compromise where possible. There are forces driving Brexit that would like to see the Transatlantic relationship unravel.

But we need each other today more than ever to protect the values we fought for together in the 20th century. It is more important now that the West stays together and does not allow us to be divided for it is our values today in a collective way that can lead the rest in a world that is more interconnected and globalized than ever, and we may want or think that globalization—some may like it and some may not.

But globalization is here and I think that we need to utilize it to bring us closer together, set standards together, and lead together from the west so that others can follow.

And with that, I yield back.

Mr. ROHRABACHER. Thanks very much, and I guess you can see where there is a difference between Republicans and Democrats on this. Just glad that the French decided to side with self-determination for our side rather than back up the British.

Ms. Kelly, please feel free.

Ms. KELLY. Thank you, Mr. Chairman, for holding a hearing on the developments of the Brexit negotiations.

Given the issues earlier this week and the negotiations, it is a particularly relevant time for this hearing. Time is passing quickly and pressure is building to get a deal done by March 2019, as you have already heard.

For the United States, there are important trade, national security, and foreign policy implications for the United Kingdom leaving the European Union.

The promises by the lead camp are likely to be broken with agreements to the European court of justice and the costs of leaving likely difficult pills to swallow.

While the U.S.-U.K. relationship is likely to change following the exit from the EU, the bond between our two nations will endure.

I look forward to hearing from the witnesses today about Brexit and the best way for Congress to plan for the future.

I yield back.

Mr. BOYLE. Yes. Well, thank you. I want to thank the chairman and the ranking member.

Before I begin, I want to acknowledge a few dignitaries with some elected officials from the Republic of Ireland who are here this week in Washington for meetings and specifically this hearing. So Senator Billy Lawless, Deputy Darragh O'Brien and Deputy Sean Barrett, you are—you are welcome here at any time in the halls of Congress.

As perhaps the chairman and ranking member may now, and certainly Chairman Royce will remember, last—in 2016 about a month or two before the Brexit vote in June 2016, I went to Chairman Royce and Ranking Member Engel and I said I would really like to—for us in the Foreign Affairs Committee to hold a hearing on Brexit.

And I think I have been pestering them every month or so since then because at the time I thought there was a much higher possibility of a vote for Brexit than was commonly thought in the mainstream media either in the U.K. or the U.S. And sure enough, by 52-48 Brexit ended up happening—one of—a couple very inter- esting and surprising election results in that year.

One of the reasons why I was so concerned about Brexit was the impact, obviously, on the U.S.-U.K. relationship, a very important relationship. Losing the U.K. as a voice at the Ryder EU table, which I believe would hurt U.S. influence, but also and especially the unintended consequence it would have on the peace process in Northern Ireland.

One of the great achievements of American, Irish, and British foreign policy, one of the few achievements in foreign policy peace processes in my lifetime has been the Northern Ireland peace process, and both Democrats and Republicans on Capitol Hill can be proud of that because we played a leading role in pushing our own

U.S. administration at the Presidential level to get diplomatically involved.

It was at the urging of Republican Congressman Pete King and Democratic Congressman Richard Neal and Joe Crowley and a number of others who have retired that President Clinton gave a visa to Gerry Adams, brought Sinn Fein into a political process.

At first it was controversial but the British eventually saw the wisdom in that. We ended up having a cease fire and, sure enough, especially through the good work of George Mitchell and the support of Dublin and London, were able to reach the Good Friday agreement.

But now because of Brexit, what for 20 years has been a seamless border, I have crossed it by accident—you can literally be driving along the road and not realize that you have crossed the border in fact a couple times—now that is suddenly all at risk, and as you may have noticed just recently as this week, you saw the—apparently, British Prime Minister Theresa May had reached an agreement only an hour later to reverse that and here we are.

So when I ask my questions I am going to focus specifically on the border issue. There are a number of very important aspects of Brexit, specifically for the United States.

And so, again, we will commend the leadership of the subcommittee for holding this hearing and I thank you.

Mr. ROHRABACHER. Well, thank you, and welcome aboard.

And a new welcome aboard, of course, was John Curtis. Do you have an opening statement for us today?

Mr. CURTIS. Thank you, Mr. Chairman.

Just briefly I do, and would like to mention due to other commitments I won't be able to answer my questions in person but would like to submit those and look forward to hearing from you.

However, I would want to make sure that I express my appreciation for me and my constituents in Utah for the great relationship that we have with the United Kingdom for the many years of history of that relationship for the mutually beneficial things that flow from that relationship and look forward to maintaining that.

In addition, hoping that as this Brexit moves forward it can be done as gracefully as possible so that we can enjoy that same relationship with others in the European Union, and thank you for being here today.

Mr. ROHRABACHER. I will now introduce our panelists and, again, thank you to each and every one of you today and, as I say, if you could put it down to about 5 minutes then we can all have a nice dialogue about the points that you've made.

So, first, what I will do is I will introduce all of you and then we will go one by one.

First we have Nile Gardiner, and he's the director of the Margaret Thatcher Center for Freedom at the Heritage Foundation, and don't let anybody every suggest because I love the Irish, as my boss, Ronald Reagan, did, that we didn't also love Margaret Thatcher. So on the record there.

Dr. Gardiner is an expert on USA-U.K. relationships and previously served as an aide to Lady Thatcher from 2000 to 2002. He earned a doctorate in history from Yale and holds degrees from Oxford University as well.

And Marjorie Chorlins—all right—as vice president for European Affairs at the U.S. Chamber of Commerce and the executive director of the U.S.-U.K. Business Council.

She has worked in both the private and public sectors with increasing seniority. She served as a deputy assistant secretary within the Commerce Department and held senior positions with Motorola as well.

She is a graduate of John Hopkins School of Advanced International Studies and Wellesley College.

Finally, we have with us Thomas Wright. He is the director of the Center on the United States and Europe at the Brookings Institute.

Previously, he was executive director at the Chicago Council on Global Affairs, a lecturer at the University of Chicago and a senior researcher for the Princeton Project on National Security.

He has earned a doctorate from Georgetown University and other degrees from Cambridge University and the University in Dublin.

Your full written statements will be made part of the record and so Mr. Gardiner, you may proceed.

STATEMENT OF NILE GARDINER, PH.D., DIRECTOR, MARGARET THATCHER CENTER FOR FREEDOM, THE HERITAGE FOUNDATION

Mr. GARDINER. Yes. Thank you. Chairman Rohrabacher, Ranking Member Meeks, and distinguished members, thank you for the opportunity to testify before your committee.

For reasons of time, I will be summarizing parts of my written statement. Today's hearing takes place at a crucially important moment for the United Kingdom, America's closest friend and ally.

On June 23rd, 2016, 17.4 million Britons voted to leave the European Union in a historic referendum with nearly 52 percent of the vote. Turnout was over 72 percent of the electorate.

A majority of the British people voted to retake control of Britain's borders, laws, trade, and destiny with an emphatic declaration of national sovereignty and self-determination.

On March 29th, 2019, Great Britain will leave the European Union and, for the first time in nearly half a century, it will be free to negotiate its own free trade deals and fully shape its own path.

Brexit offers the British people an opportunity to forge a new future as a truly global outward-looking, innovative, and prosperous world power, a standard bearer of economic freedom and liberty.

Despite the dire warnings presented by opponents of Brexit in what was dubbed Project Fear, Britain has thrived since the Brexit referendum with growing inward investment into the U.K., falling unemployment, and a soaring stock market.

The British Government is presently negotiating a post-Brexit arrangement with 27 other members of the European Union who are represented by the European Commission.

The talks, which began in June this year, have already gone through several rounds with the seventh due to take place later this month.

The negotiations are highly complex and have at times been tense, especially over the EU's financial demands, which have been rightly criticized in the U.K. in some quarters as excessive and even extortionate.

The European Commission's extremely aggressive approach is driven by several factors, including the desire to extract as much money as possible from the British people before they are freed from the shackles of the EU combined with the deep-seated hostility toward Brexit among EU officials who see it as a direct challenge to the European project.

The European Commission has taken the wrong lessons from Britain's EU exit. Brexit sent a clear message that Europe needs greater sovereignty, decentralization of power and increased political accountability.

This should be a moment for humility rather than arrogance from European Union officials. Yet, the response of European Commission President Jean-Claude Juncker has been to double down and call for even greater powers for Brussels.

His recent State of the Union address before the European Parliament was a delusional rallying cry for a Federal Europe at a time when voters across Europe are increasingly opting for a very different vision.

The EU's unelected and unaccountable ruling elites fear that Britain's exit will encourage other countries in the EU to go down the same path as the U.K.

They believe that the terms of Britain's exit must be severe and harsh in order to act as a deterrent and as a warning to others that there are major risks and consequences for going down the same path.

The European Commission's demand for a vast Brexit bill before trade talks can even begin are, in my view, mean spirited, unrealistic, and insulting.

Additionally, they are potentially an insurmountable stumbling block to any agreement being reached between London and Brussels.

If the EU continues to insist on making demands that are onerous and unacceptable, the United Kingdom should be prepared to walk away from talks with Brussels and pursue a no-deal option whereby Great Britain trades with the European Union under World Trade Organization rules.

This would be a far better course than accepting terms which are unpalatable to the British people. Britain is a global economic power, but now it conducts more business with the rest of the world than it does with the EU.

While a genuine free trade deal with the EU would be ideal, Britain can thrive and prosper if necessary without one. Britain's a huge export market for European producers and goods and services will continue to flow between the U.K. and EU regardless of whether a formal agreement is in place.

To be a truly sovereign nation, Britain must be outside of the EU single market, customs union, and the jurisdiction of the European Court of Justice. These should be clear red lines for the Brexit negotiations.

The United States has a major strategic interest in the long-term success of Brexit as well as an enduring transatlantic alliance which has remained the foundation of post-war U.S. global leadership.

An independent Britain will be a stronger ally for America than one submerged within an increasingly Federal Europe.

Britain in the Brexit era is a powerful force on the world stage, playing a leading role in bolstering NATO's eastern flank in the Baltic States, acting as the second biggest contributor to U.S.-led operations against ISIS, and preparing to launch two world-class air craft carriers, far from retreating to isolationism.

Brexit Britain is emerging as a growing force to be reckoned with across the globe. Brexit will only strengthen the transatlantic alliance rather than weaken it, leading to a more self-confident Britain that is better able to stand with the United States.

Thank you for giving me the opportunity to testify before you today. In conclusion, Britain's decision to leave the EU should be a cause for celebration here in America, and as Britain's foreign secretary, Boris Johnson, noted in his speech to the Conservative Party Conference in Manchester recently, it is time to let the British Lion roar again on the world stage, a formidable force for freedom alongside the American eagle.

Thank you.

[The prepared statement of Mr. Gardiner follows:]

CONGRESSIONAL TESTIMONY

Brexit: A Negotiation Update

Testimony of Dr. Nile Gardiner
Director, Margaret Thatcher Center for Freedom
The Heritage Foundation

Testimony before
The House Committee on Foreign Affairs Subcommittee Hearing:
Europe, Eurasia, and Emerging Threats

December 6, 2017

Chairman Rohrabacher, Ranking Member Meeks, and distinguished Members, thank you for the opportunity to testify before your committee.

Today's hearing takes place at a crucially important time for the United Kingdom, America's closest friend and ally. On June 23, 2016, 17.4 million Britons voted to leave the European Union in a historic referendum, with nearly 52 percent of the vote. Turnout was over 72 percent of the electorate. A majority of the British people voted to retake control of Britain's borders, laws, trade and destiny, with an emphatic declaration of national sovereignty and self-determination.

On March 29, 2019, Great Britain will leave the European Union, and for the first time in nearly half a century it will be free to negotiate its own free trade deals and fully shape its own path. Brexit offers the British people an opportunity to forge a new future as a truly global, outward-looking, innovative and prosperous world power, a standard bearer of economic freedom and liberty.

Despite the dire warnings presented by opponents of Brexit in what was dubbed "Project Fear," Britain has thrived since the Brexit referendum, with growing inward investment into the UK, falling unemployment, and a soaring stock market. There has been no exodus of foreign banks or a flight of international talent as critics of Brexit had warned. In the Brexit era, the City of London looks to maintain its dominance of European and global financial markets and Britain will continue to attract some of the best talent in the world. According to Dr. Liam Fox, the UK International Trade Secretary, the UK "attracted more foreign direct investment projects than ever before in the year 2016 to 2017, with more than 2,200 projects recorded."

The Brexit Negotiations

The British Government team, led by Brexit Secretary David Davis, are presently negotiating a post-Brexit arrangement with the 27 other members of the European Union. The EU's Executive Branch, the European Commission, is heading the negotiations on the European side. The European Chief Negotiator is Michel Barnier, a former French government minister.

The talks, which began in June this year, have already gone through several rounds, with a seventh due to take place later this month. Key issues of discussion between the two sides include: European Commission demands for a "divorce settlement" from Britain, with an extraordinary figure of 60 billion Euros ($70 billion) cited by Brussels; the future status of EU citizens in Britain; and the question of a "hard border" in Northern Ireland.

The negotiations are highly complex, and have at times been tense, especially over the EU's financial demands, which have been attacked in the UK as excessive and even extortionate. The European Commission's extremely aggressive approach is driven by several factors, including a desire to ruthlessly extract as much money as possible from the British people before they are freed from the shackles of the EU, combined with a deep-seated hostility towards Brexit among EU officials who see it as a direct challenge to the European Project.

The European Commission has taken the wrong lessons from Britain's EU exit. Brexit sent a clear message that Europe needs greater sovereignty, decentralization of power and increased political accountability. This should be a moment for humility rather than arrogance from European Union officials.

Yet the response of European Commission President Jean Claude Juncker has been to double down and call for even greater powers for Brussels, with his recent appeal for a "fully fledged European defense union," while warning Britain it would "regret" its decision to leave the European club. Mr. Juncker's September 2017 "State of the Union" address before the European Parliament was a delusional rallying cry for a federal Europe at a time when voters across Europe are increasingly opting for a very different vision.

The EU's unelected and unaccountable ruling elites fear that Britain's exit will encourage other countries in the European Union to go down the same path as the UK, potentially unraveling the bloc altogether. They believe that the terms of Britain's exit must be severe and harsh in order to act as a deterrent and a warning to others that there are major risks and consequences for going down the same path.

In contrast, British officials have made it abundantly clear that the United Kingdom does not seek to break up the European Union, and wishes to have a close and friendly relationship with its European neighbours after leaving the EU. The British government has argued strongly that it is in the interests of both sides to have a forward-looking trade deal that enhances investment and trade opportunities on both sides of the channel.

However, the European Commission's demand for a vast "Brexit bill" before trade talks can even begin are mean-spirited, unrealistic, and insulting. Additionally, they are a potentially insurmountable stumbling block to any agreement being reached between London and Brussels. In the words of Sir James Dyson, a leading British entrepreneur and prominent supporter of Brexit within Britain's business community, the EU's monetary demands are "outrageous," and should be rejected.

Press reports suggest that the British government may be prepared to concede a payment between £40 billion and £50 billion to the EU as a "divorce" settlement. This figure has not yet been confirmed by Downing Street and should be viewed as speculation at this time. The British government had formally offered a figure of £20 billion in September, which was rebuffed by the European Commission.

If the EU continues to insist on making demands that are onerous and unacceptable, the United Kingdom should be prepared to walk away from talks with Brussels and pursue a "no deal" option, whereby Great Britain trades with the European Union under World Trade Organisation (WTO) rules. This would be a better course than accepting terms which are unpalatable to the British people. Britain is a global economic power that now conducts more business with the rest of the world than it does with the EU. While a genuine free trade deal with the EU would be ideal, Britain can thrive and prosper if necessary without one. Britain is a huge export market for European producers, and goods and services will continue to flow between the UK and EU regardless of whether a formal agreement is in place.

It is also essential that Britain does not bow to demands for the European Court of Justice (ECJ), the EU's highest court, to retain the power to rule on the rights of EU citizens living in the UK following Brexit. This would be a violation of Britain's national sovereignty. UK courts must not be subject to the authority of a supranational European court. To be a truly sovereign nation, Britain must be outside of the single market, customs union and the ECJ. This should be a clear red line for the Brexit negotiations.

The Implications for the Transatlantic Relationship

The United States is not party to the negotiations between the European Union and the United Kingdom. But it does have a major strategic interest in the long-term success of Brexit, as well as in an enduring transatlantic alliance, which has remained the foundation of post-war US global leadership.

It is in America's interests to have a robust, powerful Special Relationship with Great Britain, one that will only be enhanced with the UK outside of the European Union. A strong independent Britain will be a better ally than one subsumed into an increasingly federal Europe.

Britain in the Brexit era is a robust force on the world stage, playing a leading role in strengthening NATO's eastern flank in the Baltic States, acting as the second biggest contributor to US-led operations against ISIS, and preparing to launch two world-class aircraft carriers. Far from retreating into isolationism, Brexit Britain is emerging as a growing force to be reckoned with across the globe.

While building an even stronger partnership with the UK, the United States will continue to strengthen ties with key allies in Europe. Regardless of the future of the European Union, alliance building with European capitals must and will be a strategic priority for Washington as it confronts an array of threats to the free world: from a resurgent Russia to the growing menace of Kim Jong-un's North Korea and the looming threat of a nuclear-armed Iran. Brexit will only strengthen the transatlantic alliance rather than weaken it, leading to a more self-confident Britain that is better able to stand with the United States.

The Importance of a US-UK Free Trade Deal

The United States should also seize upon Brexit as a tremendous opportunity to negotiate and sign a historic free trade agreement with the United Kingdom—a deal that would advance prosperity on both sides of the Atlantic. Significantly, the United States already has in place 20 Free Trade Agreements – with nations from Chile to Singapore. In contrast, the UK has not been allowed to negotiate a single trade deal on its own since it joined the European Economic Community (now EU) in 1973.

Both the United States and the United Kingdom have much to gain from a free trade deal between the world's largest and fifth largest economies. US and British negotiators should seek to agree on a trade deal that further advances economic opportunity, ideally with an agreement that eliminates all tariff barriers between the two countries.

Britain is the biggest direct foreign investor in the US and British companies employ over a million American workers. More than 1.25 million Britons are employed by US affiliates in the United Kingdom. As the Congressional Research Service notes, Britain is America's largest services trading partner, and the $5 trillion of U.S. corporate assets in the U.K. represents 22 percent of total U.S. overseas corporate assets.

A US-UK free trade deal will be a powerful force generator for economic liberty and prosperity. It will also be a dynamic symbol of the enduring ties that bind the two greatest forces for freedom in the world. Indeed, the Special Relationship will be one of the biggest beneficiaries of Brexit. And this is good news for Britain, America, and the free world.

Significantly, Britain is far more likely to get a trade deal with the United States before the supranational European Union does. The proposed US-EU Transatlantic Trade and Investment Partnership (TTIP) is, to all intents and purposes, dead in the water and has little prospect of being negotiated in the next few years.

America's Interest in a Successful Brexit

Thank you for giving me the opportunity to testify before you today. In conclusion, Britain's decision to leave the EU should be a cause for celebration here in America. Brexit embodies the very principles and ideals the American people hold dear to their hearts: self-determination, limited government, democratic accountability, and economic liberty. A truly free and powerful Great Britain is good for the United States.

Brexit will strengthen the Anglo-American Special Relationship, the most important bilateral partnership in the world. Both the Executive Branch and

Congress should give their full encouragement to the people of the United Kingdom as they forge a new path outside of the European Union.

As Britain's Foreign Secretary Boris Johnson noted in his speech to the Conservative Party Conference in Manchester, it is time to let the British Lion "roar" again on the world stage, a formidable force for freedom alongside the American Eagle.

STATEMENT OF MS. MARJORIE CHORLINS, VICE PRESIDENT FOR EUROPEAN AFFAIRS, EXECUTIVE DIRECTOR OF U.S.-U.K. BUSINESS COUNCIL, U.S. CHAMBER OF COMMERCE

Ms. CHORLINS. Thank you, Mr. Chairman and Mr. Ranking Member, distinguished members of the subcommittee, thank you very much for the opportunity to testify today on the economic impact of Brexit and how we can strengthen relationship between the U.S. and the U.K.

The Chamber established the U.S.-U.K. Business Council to provide a platform for American businesses to be heard as the U.K. resets its relationship with the EU.

Our members are eager to deepen our bilateral relationship after Brexit takes place, up to and including negotiation of a free trade agreement when the time is right.

The Council has provided inputs to Brussels and London on several issues, including the future of U.K.-EU economic relations, the urgent need for an early agreement on a transition period, and the dangers of a no-deal Brexit.

Today's hearing is another useful opportunity to ensure American investors' voices are heard. The longstanding special relationship between the U.S. and U.K. is built on deep and abiding economic and security ties.

The durability of this alliance derives from our shared commitment to rule of law, democratic norms, and free enterprise.

American companies have long looked to the U.K. as a safe and certain market. Even though the U.S. has no direct role in the negotiations between the U.K. and EU, we have a responsibility to advocate for a minimally disruptive outcome.

If Brexit is mismanaged or if the U.K. crashes out of the EU without an agreement, the economic consequences would be substantial.

As had been noted, to date progress in these complicated divorce proceedings has been limited, especially on the three primary issues of citizens' rights, border in Ireland, and the U.K.'s financial obligations.

European leaders do acknowledge that some progress is made, but as of today they believe momentum is not yet sufficient to move to discussion of the future relationship.

Our hope is that they will finally agree to move forward with that broader discussion at the European Council meeting later this month.

Still, that leaves less than a year to negotiate and ratify the final terms of the U.K.'s exit and to outline the terms of their future relationship. The clock is ticking, and time is running short.

Bilateral economic ties between the U.S. and U.K. are significant. We are each other's single largest foreign investors, and more than 2.5 million jobs depend directly on those investments.

U.S. companies have invested approximately $600 billion in the U.K., which represents nearly a quarter of U.S. investment in Europe and approximately 12 percent of all U.S. foreign investment worldwide.

British companies have invested more than $480 billion here. One point one million Americans work for these companies.

Every American state has jobs that are connected to or originated from an investment by a U.K. company. These are high quality and high-paying jobs.

The U.K. is our fourth largest export destination. U.S. goods and services exports to the U.K. exceeded $120 billion in 2016, building a $15 billion trade surplus.

Over 42,000 American firms directly export to the U.K. and more than 7,500 American companies have operations there. Given the depth of our existing relationship, the Brexit negotiations and follow-on U.K.-EU talks matter deeply for American business.

It is important to underline that much of the U.S. investment in the U.K. was made with an eye toward accessing the much larger EU single market.

A future U.K.-EU trade agreement will almost certainly not replicate the economic advantages of Britain's current membership in the single market.

For example, financial services firms are likely to lose their passporting rights to operate in all EU jurisdictions from their U.K. headquarters. Changes in the regulatory space also are anticipated. Divergences between the U.K. and EU rules will make compli- ance more difficult and expensive for U.S. companies with interests across Europe.

Digital privacy compliance mechanisms would also be in legal jeopardy if the EU and U.K. do not negotiate an agreement on data flows.

This will affect every American company that does business on either side of the English Channel. A no deal Brexit with no negotiated outcome governing the future terms of trade regulation or the movement of labor would be a disaster for U.S. companies. The consequences will be immediate and severe.

For trade, implementing the so-called "WTO option" would likely lead to sizeable losses in two-way trade and investment. The WTO has not liberalized international trade in services to nearly the same degree as the EU.

Services represent an outsized share of U.S. companies' investment in and exports from Britain. So a lack of regulatory certainty would be particularly damaging.

How many jobs will leave Britain and where they may end up is among the most difficult changes to predict. Many companies are understandably waiting for further clarity before green lighting any new investments in the U.K.

American investors have developed worst case contingency plans, which they may be forced to execute if clarity isn't forthcoming quickly.

Even as the Brexit negotiations play out, the U.K. is and will remain a vital economic partner for the United States. The U.K. has a talented English-speaking and tech savvy workforce.

Its government has traditionally preferred a regulatory model that rewards innovation and encourages competition, much like the American model.

The U.K. has been a consistent advocate for the digital economy, ensuring regulatory decisions are fact based and rely on sound science and has supported a predictable and transparent business climate.

While we will miss that voice in Brussels, the U.K.'s departure creates opportunities for the U.S. to strengthen our bilateral ties, up to and including a possible free trade agreement when the time is right.

Any commercially meaningful U.S.-U.K. agreement should focus heavily on the services sector and also on setting global standards in important areas such as digital trade, regulatory cooperation, investment protection, promoting trade opportunities for small and medium sized enterprises, competition, and treatment of state-owned enterprises.

While traditional market access barriers are low between the U.S. and U.K., removing all tariffs would still yield significant benefits.

This is especially true for small companies for which a 5 percent tariff or an extra customs form may be the difference between a profitable sale and a missed opportunity.

In closing, even as we pursue closer U.S.-U.K. ties, strengthening our ties with the rest of Europe also must remain a priority.

The U.S. has promoted a more integrated European market for the past seven decades. This has proven tremendously successful for the transatlantic alliance and for American companies that do business in Europe.

With that in mind, we must ultimately endeavor to deepen trade and investment ties with both Britain and the EU in the years ahead.

Thank you.

[The prepared statement of Ms. Chorlins follows:]

Statement of the U.S. Chamber of Commerce

ON: The Challenges of Brexit and the Opportunities of an Expanded U.S.-UK Economic Relationship

**TO: U.S. House Foreign Affairs Committee
Subcommittee on Europe, Eurasia, and Emerging Threats**

**BY: Marjorie Chorlins
Vice President, European Affairs
Executive Director, U.S.-UK Business Council
U.S. Chamber of Commerce**

DATE: December 6, 2017

1615 H Street NW | Washington, DC | 20062

The U.S. Chamber of Commerce is the world's largest business federation representing the interests of more than 3 million businesses of all sizes, sectors, and regions, as well as state and local chambers and industry associations. The Chamber is dedicated to promoting, protecting, and defending America's free enterprise system.

More than 96% of Chamber member companies have fewer than 100 employees, and many of the nation's largest companies are also active members. We are therefore cognizant not only of the challenges facing smaller businesses, but also those facing the business community at large.

Besides representing a cross-section of the American business community with respect to the number of employees, major classifications of American business—e.g., manufacturing, retailing, services, construction, wholesalers, and finance—are represented. The Chamber has membership in all 50 states.

The Chamber's international reach is substantial as well. We believe that global interdependence provides opportunities, not threats. In addition to the American Chambers of Commerce abroad, an increasing number of our members engage in the export and import of both goods and services and have ongoing investment activities. The Chamber favors strengthened international competitiveness and opposes artificial U.S. and foreign barriers to international business.

Introduction

Good afternoon, Mr. Chairman and distinguished members of the subcommittee. My name is Marjorie Chorlins, and I serve as Vice President for European Affairs at the U.S. Chamber of Commerce and Executive Director of the Chamber's U.S.-UK Business Council. Thank you for this opportunity to testify on the economic impacts of Brexit and opportunities to strengthen the economic relationship between the U.S. and the United Kingdom.

The Chamber established the U.S.-UK Business Council to provide a platform for American businesses to be heard as the UK resets its relationship with the EU and its position in the global economy. We have provided input to Brussels and London on our priorities for future UK-EU economic relations; the urgent need for a transition period to give business and governments the time needed to adjust to the new circumstances; and the dangers of a "no deal" Brexit. These reports are appended to our written testimony, and I appreciate their inclusion in the record.

The longstanding 'special relationship' between the United States and the United Kingdom is built on deep and abiding economic, foreign policy, and security ties. The durability of this alliance derives from the two countries' shared commitment to rule of law, democratic norms, and free enterprise. American companies have looked to the UK as a safe and certain market in an increasingly uncertain world.

Brexit has the potential to disrupt the geopolitical and strategic relationship between key American allies in Europe. We are encouraged that both the EU and the UK have consistently stressed the need for continued intelligence sharing and security cooperation, even after the UK leaves the EU. A fractured and distracted Europe is in no one's best interest, particularly at a time when we face significant threats to our shared security and joint prosperity.

Similarly, If Brexit is mismanaged, or if the UK crashes out of the EU without an agreement on their future relationship, the economic consequences would be substantial, and thousands of U.S. firms and their employees would be directly affected.

The Depth of the U.S.-UK Special Economic Relationship

Brexit matters because the economic ties U.S. and the UK are deep and enduring. We are each other's single largest foreign investors, and more than 2.5 million jobs depend directly on those investments. Two-way trade totals more than $235 billion annually.

U.S. companies have invested approximately $600 billion in the UK, which represents nearly a quarter of U.S. investment in Europe, and approximately 12% of all U.S. foreign investment worldwide. This investment directly employs nearly 1.4 million Britons and millions more indirectly.

Similarly, the United States has greatly benefitted from British investment across the country. More than 1.1 million Americans work for British companies in the U.S., and British companies have invested more than $480 billion here. This accounts for more than 15% of all foreign investment into the U.S.

Every American state has jobs that are connected to, or originated from, an investment by a UK company. California, New York, Texas, Pennsylvania, and Illinois are the five states with the most employment by British firms. American jobs supported by British investment are high quality and highly paid—in manufacturing, chemicals, pharmaceuticals, information technology, and financial services, among other sectors.

Mr. Chairman, according to the British Embassy, UK companies directly employ more than 98,000 people in California, and California's exports to the UK support an additional 105,000 jobs. Mr. Ranking Member, New York has over 103,000 employees of British firms, while New York exports to the UK support an additional 81,000 jobs.

In terms of trade, the UK is our 4th largest export destination, and our 7th largest trading partner overall for goods and services. U.S. goods and services exports to the UK total about $121 billion, yielding a $15 billion U.S. trade surplus. Today, over 42,000 American firms directly export to the UK, and more than 7,500 American companies have operations in the UK.

It is also worth comparing U.S. investments in the UK with investments in other countries. Of note, as of 2016, U.S. companies had invested only 13% as much in China as they have in the United Kingdom.

Obviously, it is in our national interest to build on this solid foundation and work to further strengthen our commercial relationship, up to and including negotiation of a bilateral free trade agreement when the time is right.

Brexit: Where Are We and What's Next?

In March 2017, the UK started a two-year countdown clock to exiting the European Union. As the subcommittee knows, this complicated "divorce" proceeding is politically sensitive on both sides of the English Channel. The level of complexity in unwinding more than 40 years of economic, strategic, and political union should not be underestimated. Pursuant to the terms of Article 50 of the European Union treaties, Britain will no longer be a member of the European Union as of March 29, 2019. Were the UK to arrive at that date without agreement on at least the framework of the new UK-EU trade relationship, the disruption in UK-EU ties—and the attendant effects on U.S. companies—would be devastating.

With that in mind, we have called on negotiators to agree to a transition period of no less than three years during which the UK would continue to operate under EU rules while the two sides negotiate a comprehensive trade agreement.

To date, progress at the negotiating table has been limited. The Europeans have identified three areas where "sufficient progress" must be made before negotiations can commence on the future UK-EU trade relationship. These areas include treatment of EU citizens living and working in the UK and vice versa; how to manage the border between Northern Ireland and the rest of Ireland once the UK exits; and agreement on the UK's financial obligations in light of previously agreed spending commitments.

In October, the European Council, comprised of EU heads of state and government, noted that while some progress has been made on each of these issues, it is not yet sufficient to move to the second phase of negotiations.[1] European leaders did, however, instruct the European Commission to begin internal preparations for discussions towards a future trade agreement with the UK. Our hope is that the Council will agree to move forward with this broader discussion at its meeting later this month, on December 14-15. It seems like a potential compromise may be within reach, but the deal has not yet been finalized.

Still, even if the UK and the EU agree to move on to the trade talks later this month, that would give the two sides less than a year to negotiate the final terms of the UK's exit and to outline the terms of their future relationship, including security cooperation, research and development, trade, investment, and regulatory cooperation. The negotiating window is narrow given the amount of time it will take to have the agreement ratified.

Why Does Brexit Matter to the U.S. Business Community?

Given the extent of our existing relationships, Brexit matters deeply for American business. It is important to underline that much of the U.S. investment in the UK was made so companies could seamlessly access the much larger EU Single Market.

A future UK-EU trade agreement will almost certainly not replicate the economic advantages of Britain's current membership in the Single Market. For example, financial services firms are likely to lose their "passporting" rights to operate in all EU jurisdictions from their UK European headquarters. This would similarly affect companies whose headquarters are in other EU member states in terms of their ability to do business in the UK.

Changes in the regulatory space are also anticipated. Since the UK does not have its own fully-functioning regulatory agencies covering important sectors like pharmaceuticals or aviation, it will likely remain reliant on, and subject to, EU rules for at least the foreseeable future. Once outside the EU, the UK will need to develop its own regulatory regimes and hire and train new regulators. A lack of clarity as this shift occurs is among the most important concerns of many companies.

Digital privacy compliance mechanisms could also be in legal jeopardy if the EU and UK do not negotiate an agreement on data flows or if, for example, the UK no longer qualifies for data transfers under the rules of the U.S.-EU Privacy Shield arrangement. This will negatively affect every American company that does business on either side of the English Channel, and costs will rise for consumers who use the goods and services that these companies provide.

---

[1] European Council Conclusions, October 20, 2017. http://www.consilium.europa.eu/en/press/press-releases/2017/10/20/euco-art50-conclusions/

In the case of aviation, once Brexit occurs, the UK will need to have in place revised Open Skies aviation agreements with both the United States and with the EU. Otherwise, flights stop on day one—until a new agreement can be negotiated. We understand the U.S. government and UK government are already negotiating to maintain this access moving forward, which is an important step in the right direction.

The prospect of a "no deal" Brexit, with no negotiated outcome governing the future terms of trade, regulatory oversight, or the movement of labor, would be a disaster for U.S. companies. If no exit agreement is reached, the consequences will be both immediate and severe.

For trade, implementing the so-called default World Trade Organization (WTO) option would likely lead to sizeable losses in two-way trade and investment. Of note, the WTO has not liberalized international trade in services to nearly the same degree as the Single Market. That matters in an economy like Britain's where more than 80% of jobs and GDP are in the services sector. Since services represent an outsized share of U.S. companies' investment and exports from Britain, a lack of equivalent market access would be particularly damaging in this area.

On goods, WTO-level tariff increases will lead to rising costs for businesses and consumers on a range of everyday necessities, such as food and medicine.

Additionally, the UK's independent membership in the WTO is contingent on all WTO members signing up to its revised tariff schedules and tariff-rate quotas as agreed with the EU. A wide range of agricultural exporters including the U.S., Australia, Argentina, Brazil, and New Zealand have already objected to the EU and UK's initial offer on the latter.

Additional costs also will be incurred by major delays at the border. In fact, the UK's customs authority estimates indicate that customs declarations at ports like Dover will increase fivefold, from 55 million annually to over 255 million per year.[2] It is difficult to imagine how Britain's ports or the Channel Tunnel will be able to handle the dramatically increased traffic and customs requirements as the UK exits the EU. There is also a lack of skilled talent to fill the dozens of additional customs clearance positions which will be needed post-Brexit. Significant delays at the border would directly harm U.S. manufacturers that depend on seamless supply chains that often require multiple border crossings from Europe into the UK and vice versa.

Consumers will also face increased costs. Pallets, containers, and crates that carry automotive parts, fresh fruit and vegetables, and fast-moving consumer goods will be subject to tariffs not applied today, which will raise costs on essentials in Britain and beyond. This will directly impact the bottom line for U.S. firms in the manufacturing, retail, and logistics sectors.

How Could Brexit Impact Jobs and Investment?

---

[2] HMRC Chief Warns post-Brexit Border and Tax Checks Could Cost up to £800 million. The Guardian. https://www.theguardian.com/politics/2017/sep/14/hmrc-chief-warns-post-brexit-border-and-tax-checks-could-cost-up-to-800m

The tremendous uncertainty surrounding Brexit and the UK's future relationship with the EU is already having a negative effect on the business climate. A study in October revealed that fully 82% of foreign businesses operating in Britain, including American ones, are either "not very" or "not at all confident" that a positive outcome for the UK can be achieved in the Brexit negotiations. Similarly, 55% of these companies think Brexit will have a negative impact on their future investments in the UK.

Without knowing the terms of the future UK-EU relationship, it is difficult to quantify the potential jobs impact. What we do know is that for U.S. financial services firms with European headquarters in London, losing passporting rights will require them to shift at least some positions to other EU member states. Other firms are awaiting further clarity before green-lighting new investments in the UK. American investors also have developed worst case contingency plans, which they may be forced to execute if clarity isn't forthcoming soon. All of these developments have potential job impacts.

How Can the U.S. Strengthen Ties to a Post-Brexit United Kingdom?

Regardless of the future of UK-EU relations, the UK is and will remain a vital economic partner for the United States. The UK has a talented, English-speaking, and tech-savvy workforce. Its government has traditionally preferred a regulatory model that rewards innovation and encourages competition—much like the American model. The UK has been one of the most forward-leaning voices in Europe on key issues such as promoting the digital economy, ensuring regulatory decisions are fact-based and rest on sound science, and supporting a predictable and transparent business climate.

It is essential that we build on our existing relationship, and we should explore all options including a possible bilateral free trade agreement with the UK when the time is right. To that end, we appreciate, the preliminary work being done under the auspices of a newly-formed U.S.-UK Trade and Investment Working Group.

For now, the focus of the business community must be on the UK-EU negotiations. At present, the UK is still subject to the EU's Common Commercial Policy, making it unable to negotiate its own bilateral trade agreements. Secondly, the UK government's limited trade negotiating resources are largely focused on the EU discussions. Lastly, it is impossible to gauge the potential terms of a bilateral U.S.-UK agreement until we know what the UK and EU have agreed in terms of market access and regulatory oversight. It's possible the EU will seek commitments that limit what the UK can do with third countries in the future.

What we do know already is that any commercially meaningful U.S.-UK agreement should focus heavily on the services sector and on setting global standards in important areas like digital trade, regulatory cooperation, investment protection, creating opportunities for small and medium-sized enterprises, competition, and treatment of state-owned enterprises.

While traditional market access barriers are low between the U.S. and UK, removing all tariffs would still yield significant benefits. This is especially true for small companies for which a 5% tariff or an extra customs form may be the difference between a profitable sale and a missed opportunity.

Finally, it is important to underline that even as the U.S. moves to expand its trade and investment ties with the UK post-Brexit, strengthening our economic ties with the rest of Europe must remain a top priority. For over 70 years, the United States has actively pursued a more integrated Europe and this has proven beneficial in both national security and commercial terms. With that in mind, we should endeavor to deepen our trade and investment ties with both Britain and the EU in the years ahead.

Conclusion

I would like to thank the Subcommittee for the opportunity to testify today. The U.S. business community is eager to be heard during the Brexit negotiations, and to play a productive role in deepening the 'special relationship' between our two countries. The Chamber and its members look forward to working closely with the Congress to achieve these goals.

Attachments to Testimony

I would like to submit the following with my statement:

1) *Priorities for a New EU-UK Economic Partnership*
   https://www.uschamber.com/report/priorities-new-eu-uk-economic-partnership

2) *The Future of UK-EU Relations: Priorities of the U.S. Business Community*
   https://www.uschamber.com/report/the-future-uk-eu-relations-priorities-the-us-business-community

3) *Toward a New UK-EU Relationship: The Importance of Transitional Arrangements*
   https://www.uschamber.com/report/toward-new-uk-eu-relationship-the-importance-transitional-arrangements

4) *Brexit: Deal or No Deal? Business Stresses Need for Negotiated Agreement*
   https://www.uschamber.com/issue-brief/brexit-deal-or-no-deal-business-stresses-need-negotiated-agreement

5) *Business Needs Clear Progress from Brexit Negotiators*
   https://www.uschamber.com/above-the-fold/business-needs-clear-progress-brexit-negotiators

6) *U.S.-UK Business Council Welcomes PM May's Latest Remarks on Brexit*
   https://www.uschamber.com/press-release/us-chamber-s-us-uk-business-council-welcomes-prime-minister-may-s-latest-remarks

7) *Brexit Begins: Business Seeks Open Minds, Clarity on Way Forward*
   https://www.uschamber.com/above-the-fold/brexit-begins-business-seeks-open-minds-clarity-way-forward

8) *7 Things the U.S. Business Community Wants from the Brexit Negotiations*
   https://www.uschamber.com/above-the-fold/7-things-the-us-business-community-wants-brexit-negotiations

9) *The Challenges of Brexit and the Case for a U.S.-UK Trade Agreement*
   https://www.uschamber.com/above-the-fold/the-challenges-brexit-and-the-case-us-uk-trade-agreement

Mr. ROHRABACHER. Thank you very much.

And Dr. Wright.

STATEMENT OF THOMAS WRIGHT, PH.D., DIRECTOR, CENTER ON THE UNITED STATES AND EUROPE, BROOKINGS INSTITUTION

Mr. WRIGHT. Thank you.

Chairman Rohrabacher, Ranking Member Meeks, and distinguished members, thank you for the opportunity to testify in front of this committee.

We are gathered here at a crucial moment in the history of postwar Europe. The U.K.'s decision to exit the EU I think is the most significant and important decision it has taken since the end of the Cold War. It raises fundamental questions about Europe's future and the United States has a vital interest in how these questions are resolved.

In my written testimony, I provide my analysis of where the negotiations stand and where I think they are likely to end up.

I believe there will eventually be a deal largely along the lines laid out by the EU side and I am happy to elaborate that in the questions.

But I would like to use the time allotted to me to speak now about American interests in U.S. policy in the Brexit process.

In my view, if Brexit is going to occur, the United States has a vital interest in a Brexit that produces as strong and as prosperous a U.K. as possible and as strong and as prosperous an EU as possible, working closely with each other and with America.

This should be the organizing principle of U.S. policy toward Brexit. We should actively consider any steps that can facilitate this outcome and we should oppose any steps that undermine it.

With that in mind, I am concerned by the current policy pursued by the Trump administration. The Trump administration has supported Brexit rhetorically put in practice it has done the U.K. few favors.

Just two quick examples—in a major speech on U.S.-U.K. relations in November, the U.S. Secretary of Commerce Wilbur Ross made it clear that if the U.K. wanted a free trade agreement with the U.S., the U.K. would have to choose between the United States and the EU. The U.K. would have to choose U.S. regulatory standards and diverge from those of the EU.

Secretary Ross' logic is clear. The U.K. is in a weak position and needs trade deals with third parties so the United States can afford to take a maximist position in negotiations.

Second example—at the World Trade Organization in October, the Trump administration sided with Brazil and other countries to oppose a deal already reached between the U.K. and the EU to divide agricultural import quotas between then, greatly complicating Britain's diplomacy.

More generally, the Trump administration has pursued a very passive approach to the negotiations. It sees it purely as an internal issue and has not identified any U.S. equities including maintaining the Good Friday agreement, preserving security cooperation between the U.K. and EU 27, or ensuring there is a negotiated settlement between the parties.

On the contrary, it has given the impression that the U.K. and the EU's problems may present the United States with immediate opportunities.

I am in favor of closer economic ties between the U.S. and the U.K. But at this time, I do not believe that Washington and London should pursue a bilateral FTA along the lines of that proposed by Secretary Ross and the Trump administration.

There are very few tariffs between the U.S. and U.K. so any FTA would have to focus primarily on regulatory standards.

The Trump administration's current policy is to use all of the leverage at its disposal including the threat of tariffs to compel the U.K. to diverge from the EU regulations and adopt ours.

That, I think, has two problems. The first is that the negotiations are unlikely to succeed on these terms and will alienate much of the U.K. population. I can expand more on that later.

The second and I think even more critical problem is that in the unlikely event that they do succeed on the terms set by Secretary Ross, they will by definition reduce the U.K.'s trade access to the EU. The more the U.K. diverges from the EU regulatory standards the less assess they will have to the single market.

The next effect of this will be to damage the economy of the U.K. and the EU, which will also damage U.S. economic and strategic interests.

It should be noted that closer economic ties between the U.K. and the EU is, as close as possible, is the official position of the U.K. Government, which is seeking a comprehensive trade deal. They should be free to do so without being pressured and by the United States.

And more generally, the U.S. should make it clear to the U.K. and the EU that it favors a negotiated agreement. We can live with almost any deal acceptable to both parties but a Brexit without a deal would not be in our interests.

The United States—finally, as I am running out of time, I would like to say a word about Northern Ireland. We are approaching the 20th anniversary of the Good Friday agreement, an agreement, as members have noted, that many Americans on both sides of the aisle have helped to bring about and sustain.

It is absolutely necessary for the United States to remain engaged on preserving the peace in Northern Ireland. I elaborate this—on this in my written testimony but suffice to say here that this peace I think is threatened by the current state of the negotiations.

If there is not a special—a consideration for Northern Ireland to ensure that there is an open border I think it does put the Good Friday agreement at risk.

As a first step, the Trump administration should immediately reinstate the position of special envoy for Northern Ireland, which I understand was abolished by Secretary Tillerson along with other envoys and prioritize and preserving—and preserving the Good Friday agreement should also be in issue in relations with the U.K. and the EU.

Thank you very much.

[The prepared statement of Mr. Wright follows:]

Brexit: A Negotiation Update

Testimony by
Dr. Thomas Wright
Director, Center for the U.S. and Europe, and Senior Fellow
The Brookings Institution

Hearing by the
Subcommittee on Europe, Europe and Emerging Threats
of the
Committee on Foreign Affairs
U.S. House of Representatives

December 6, 2017

Chairman Rohrabacher, Ranking Member Meeks, and distinguished Members; thank you for the opportunity to testify before your committee.

We are gathered here at a crucial moment in the history of post-war Europe. The United Kingdom's (UK) decision to exit the European Union (EU) is the most important and significant decision it has taken since the end of the Cold War. It raises fundamental questions about Europe's future. The United States has a vital interest in how these questions are resolved.

My testimony is in four parts:
I.   A status update on the Brexit negotiations
II.   The geopolitical effects of Brexit
III.   The Trump administration's approach to Brexit
IV.   US interests and policy recommendations

I: A Status Update on Brexit Negotiations
The UK government invoked Article 50 of the EU treaties on March 29, 2017. This set in motion a two-year negotiation on the terms of Britain's exit from the EU. Regardless of whether or not an agreement is reached, and barring an unexpected political sea change, Britain will formally exit on March 29, 2019.

The range of possible outcomes to the negotiations is bound by two political realities:
- The UK government has made it clear it intends to leave the EU Single Market and the Customs Union, which provides for the free movement of goods, people, services, and capital and a common tariffs to the rest of the world. This has become a political imperative, particularly for the Conservative Party.
- The EU has made it clear that if the UK leaves the Single Market and Customs Union, it will lose access to both. The UK cannot have a bespoke agreement whereby it cherry picks which regulations it will follow and the access it prefers. On this, the EU is unyielding.

The UK government had hoped that the fact that the EU 27 (the 27 countries that will remain in the EU after Britain leaves) has a trade surplus with the UK would cause them to make concessions in the negotiation, but it has not. Instead of potential narrow economic gains, the EU has prioritized political issues such as the integrity of the Single Market and the unity of the 27 in much the same way that the UK has privileged political goals, such as controlling borders, over GDP growth.

The UK has emerged as the weaker party in the negotiations. It is significantly smaller than the EU 27 and it has more at stake. It was also not prepared for the enormous complexity of the challenge, meaning that it had no clear plan, nor the technical resources to meet that challenge. By contrast, the EU 27 is united around a single set of objectives.

The effect of the disparity has been noticeable. The UK government has made, and continues to make, significant concessions to the EU in pursuit of a deal. The negotiations are in two phases. Phase 1 requires agreement on three issues—the financial settlement for exiting, citizens' rights for EU-27 citizens in the UK and UK citizens in the EU-27, and preserving the peace in Northern Ireland. The UK government has acceded to the EU's demands on the first two. At the time of writing, agreement is also close on the matter of the Irish border, which has been delayed because of the opposition of the Democratic Unionist Party, which has a confidence and supply agreement with Theresa May's government, providing it with crucial support to maintain a governing majority in Parliament.

There is no reason to believe this dynamic will change in Phase II which deals with the future relationship and the transition period. The most likely outcome is a political declaration endorsing a Canada-style free trade agreement that would significantly reduce UK access to the EU market and an association agreement covering political and security affairs. A Canada-style free trade agreement will take several additional years to agree to and will require ratification in each member state, including by referendum in some cases. In the intervening period, the UK may be subject to a transition period, the details of which will be negotiated, whereby it has to abide by all, or nearly all, of the EU's rules without any formal influence.

Two other outcomes are possible by March 29 2019. There could be a breakdown of negotiations and exit without any deal. In my view, this would only occur if hardliners in the Conservative Party bring down Theresa May as Prime Minister because they are dissatisfied with the concessions she makes. The other outcome is that the UK government could change its position and either agree to stay in the Single Market and Customs Union or to reverse Brexit entirely. My assessment is that this is the least likely outcome and it would only occur after a change in government.

II: The Geopolitical Consequences of Brexit

Ultimately, the UK and the EU 27 are wealthy and capable countries that should be able to deal with the costs and challenges of Brexit. However, in the intervening period between now and then, Brexit is likely to have several deleterious effects on the European order.

<u>Brexit is likely to damage the UK and the EU economically</u>
The UK is terminating its access to the world's largest economic bloc and is proposing to embark on trade talks around the world at a time when protectionist sentiment is at a post-Cold War high. It is hard to imagine any scenario in which the UK has greater access to global markets than it does now. London will be diminished as a financial center because it will lose the ability to provide some financial services for the EU. Some advocates of Brexit argue that it can make up some of this lost ground with a program of deregulation but it is unlikely that this approach would secure sufficient domestic support or that it would be consistent with terms negotiated with the EU to maintain

market access. Indeed, the converse is also possible—leaving the EU would allow a future Labour government led by Jeremy Corbyn to increase regulations beyond what is allowed by the EU.

Brexit will also damage the EU. The EU enjoys a trade surplus with the UK. A hard Brexit will almost certainly hit EU exports, though some EU countries will be affected more than others. Individual European cities may pick up some investment from the relative decline of the City of London but none of them enjoy its inherent advantages. The result is likely to be that the EU cannot fully replace the City of London and is diminished as a financial power. Finally, the UK has pushed the EU in a market-friendly direction over the past four decades. Without the UK, the internal balance of power may shift in a protectionist direction and towards a more "social capitalism" model than has been the case with the UK at the table.

Brexit will change dynamics inside the EU
It is possible that without the UK the EU 27 will be free to pursue a new round of political and economic integration. This appears to be the view of France's president Emmanuel Macron. However, it is also true that the UK was not the only obstacle to more integration. The EU 27 is deeply divided in what form future integration should take, particularly on Eurozone governance and migration. Moreover, with the departure of the UK, we are likely to see a greater structural tension between the Eurozone 19 and the rest of the EU 27. Greater integration will occur within the Eurozone, reducing the influence of non-Eurozone member states. As long as the UK was a member of the EU, it was difficult to sidestep. Without the weight of the UK, non-Eurozone member states may be further marginalized. The UK's departure also shifts the balance of power within the EU and heightens concerns about the extent of German influence over the European project.

Brexit puts the Good Friday Agreement (GFA) at risk
Northern Ireland's future has emerged as one of the most difficult issues in the Brexit negotiations. The EU 27 argues that there is no way for the UK to leave the Single Market and Customs Union without the imposition of a "hard border" between Northern Ireland and the Republic of Ireland. London insists it has no intention of imposing a hard border under any circumstances so the issue is much ado about nothing. However, given the terms of its leaving the EU and its presumed new role as a "third country" it could be compelled to even if it has no desire to do so. If the UK government simply kept the border open with no trade deal or a deal short of its current access to the Single Market, it would be in violation of the World Trade Organization's Most Favored Nation clause and would be subject to legal action. The closer the issue is examined the more complicated it becomes. A recent study by the EU Commission and the UK government identified 142 areas of cross-border activities, from health care to agriculture, that would be detrimentally impacted by Brexit. The net effect of a hard Brexit could be the reimposition of a hard border, an end to most of the cross border cooperation provided for under the GFA, and the erosion of the hard won peace.

Brexit could hurt the Transatlantic Alliance
By weakening the UK and the EU, Brexit diminishes the transatlantic community at a time when it is facing major challenges from a revisionist Russia, a more assertive and mercantilist China, the unraveling of regional order in the Middle East, and the persistent threat of terrorism. Europe has been a key ally in maintaining the postwar international order but now it is likely to have much narrower and more nationalistic understandings of its interest. Individual states, including the UK, may be increasingly receptive to accommodating China. They may be less willing to send troops to

address common threats. And, there may be a weakening of formal cooperation on political and security affairs which currently takes place under the auspices of the EU.

III: The Trump Administration's Approach to Brexit

The Trump Administration has supported Brexit rhetorically but in practice it has done the UK few favors. Instead, the Trump Administration appears to be pursuing a predatory policy, designed to take immediate economic advantage of the dislocations and vulnerabilities created for the UK by the Brexit process.

In a major speech on US-UK relations on November 6 2017, the US Secretary of Commerce, Wilbur Ross, made it clear that if it wanted a Free Trade Agreement (FTA) with the US, the UK would have to choose between it and the EU. He said that the UK must accept US regulatory standards and diverge from those of the EU. US regulatory standards, particularly on agricultural products, are politically controversial in the UK. And, diverging from EU regulations will, by definition, weaken the trading relationship between the UK and the EU. But Secretary Ross's logic is clear: the UK is in a weak position and needs trade deals with third parties so the United States can take a maximalist position in negotiations.

This approach has also manifested itself in US actions at the World Trade Organization. In October 2017, the Trump Administration sided with Argentina, Brazil, and other countries to oppose a deal reached between the UK and the EU to divide agricultural import quotas between them. The Trump administration is demanding that the UK unilaterally open up its agricultural markets, providing the rest of the WTO with similar access to the EU, before any trade deals are negotiated and agreed.

The Trump Administration also proposed tariffs of 220% on Bombardier, a Canadian aerospace company that employs over 4000 people in Northern Ireland. The UK government has accused the Trump Administration of protectionism and, ironically, the EU has backed the UK position. Setting aside the rights and wrongs of this particular case, it is highly likely that after Brexit the Trump Administration will lean more heavily on the UK to bend to its will in trade disputes, using its greater size as leverage.

More generally, the Trump Administration has adopted a very passive approach to the negotiations. It sees it purely as an internal UK/EU issue. It has not identified any US equities, such as maintaining the Good Friday Agreement, preserving security cooperation between the UK and the EU 27, or ensuring there is a negotiated agreement between the parties. On the contrary, it has given the impression that Europe's problems may present the US with opportunities.

IV: U.S. Interests and Policy Recommendations

In my view, if Brexit is going to occur, the US has a vital interest in a Brexit that produces as strong and prosperous a UK as possible and as strong and prosperous an EU as possible, working closely with each other and with America. This should be the organizing principle of US policy toward Brexit. We should actively consider any steps that can facilitate this outcome and we should oppose any that undermine it.

I am in favor of closer economic ties between the US and the UK but, at this time, I do not believe Washington and London should pursue a bilateral FTA along the lines of that proposed by the Trump administration. There are very few tariffs between the US and the UK so any FTA would have to focus primarily on regulatory standards. The Trump administration's current policy seems to be to use all of its leverage, including the threat of tariffs, to compel the UK to diverge from EU regulations and adopt ours. This has two problems.

The first problem is that such negotiations are unlikely to succeed and could alienate much of the UK population. For instance, the Trump administration's focus on agricultural standards in July talks with the UK caused a split in the UK cabinet and resulted in a statement by the Trade Secretary Liam Fox that the FTA would focus on services, not agriculture. However, harmonizing regulations on services, such as the financial industry or health, is likely to prove to be even more difficult and controversial. Meanwhile, the US maintains that the FTA must include UK agreement to accept US agricultural standards. The long-term health of the US-UK alliance is best-served by ensuring that any FTA enjoys enduring and broad based support in both countries. Otherwise, it will not be ratified and will only succeed in injecting distrust and disharmony into the relationship.

The second problem is that in the unlikely event that the negotiations do succeed on the terms set by Secretary Ross they will, by definition, reduce the UK's trade access to the EU. The more the UK diverges from EU regulatory standards, the less access they will have to the Single Market. The net effect of this would be to damage the economy of the UK and the EU, which would also damage US economic and strategic interests over the medium and long term.

America's long-term national interest is to facilitate as close an economic relationship as possible between the UK and the EU, to the extent desired by both parties. This, it should be noted, is also the official position of the UK government, which is seeking a comprehensive trade deal with the EU. If the UK government decides to diverge from EU regulations and reduce its access to the Single Market, it is free to do so of its own accord but it should be pressured to do so by the Trump Administration. Forcing the UK to choose between the US and the EU undermines the prospect of a smooth and mutually beneficial Brexit. The UK is not an easy mark. It is America's closest ally and should be treated as such.

More generally, the US should make it clear to the UK and the EU that it favors a negotiated agreement. We can live with almost any deal acceptable to both parties but Brexit without a deal would not be in our interests. A UK exit without a deal could inflict significant damage on the UK and EU economies, and hence on the global economy. It would sow the seeds of discord in Europe and would inhibit cooperation on issues of vital interest to the US.

After an agreement is reached, the US should engage with the UK and explore ways of deepening economic ties between the two countries in a way that does not jeopardize the UK's core economic interest in maintaining a close trading relationship with the EU. If this takes the form of trade talks, it may make sense to pursue this on a trilateral basis, by revitalizing the Transatlantic Trade and Investment Partnership (TTIP) with the EU and expanding it to include the UK. As a side note, if there is a revitalization of a transatlantic trade deal along the lines of TTIP, it would not make sense for the UK to adapt to US regulatory standards, while these are being renegotiated by the US.

The US should also increase its diplomatic engagement with the EU after Britain leaves. The EU is a vital partner of the United States in using and deploying economic power, such as sanctions. NATO, by contrast, has no economic capability. The stability and success of the Eurozone is also closely linked to the stability of the global economy and is a key part of preventing a new financial crisis. And, the EU plays an important role in upholding democracy and human rights in Europe, including against Russian interference.

Finally, as we are approaching the 20th anniversary of the GFA, an agreement many Americans on both sides of the aisle helped to bring about and sustain, it is absolutely necessary for the US to remain engaged on preserving the peace in Northern Ireland. As a first step, the Trump Administration should immediately reinstate the position of Special Envoy for Northern Ireland. Prioritizing and preserving the GFA should also be an issue in relations with the UK and the EU.

END

Mr. ROHRABACHER. Thank you all very much for your testimony, and let's just—what I am going to do is I am going to make sure my colleagues—you know what I am going to do?

I know that you have a special place in your heart for Ireland, just from what you've said, so I am going to give you a chance to talk about the Irish part of this right now before we ask the rest of our questions. You can be the lead off guy.

Mr. BOYLE. Thank you. You are very gracious and thank the indulgence of my colleagues.

Dr. Wright, I wanted to follow up and actually this is a perfect segue because you just completed on this. I noticed in your written testimony you mentioned the recent study by the U.K. Government and the EU Commission which identified—and this was, frankly, a higher number than even I expected—the U.K. Government EU Commission report identified a 142 areas of cross-border activities, from health care to agriculture, which I was familiar with. There are 142 areas, all of which would be detrimentally impacted by Brexit.

Could you expand on the findings of the report specifically as it relates to the border communities, whether they are—regardless of which side of the border they currently sit on?

Mr. WRIGHT. Yes. The study showed that the cross-border cooperation that was provided for under the Good Friday agreement really rests on regulatory alignment between the Republic of Ireland and Northern Ireland.

So the fact that they have the same regulations on agriculture, on health, on these wide array of issues, means that that they are able to cooperate on these issues, and in the aggregate this really, I think, has had a very progressive impact in terms of the peace process. It has built trust across the two communities and across the border. If there is significant divergence in regulations all of those areas of cooperation, my understanding is, either come to an end or are significantly reduced.

And so the Irish Government and the EU 27 and the British Government I think are concerned by the broader impact of Brexit on Northern Ireland separately than the border issue which, of course, is also a very severe issue with major implications.

Mr. BOYLE. I'll just share one specific anecdote that I just heard the other day that crystalizes part of what you're talking about.

The Irish Government funds a world class cancer research center and in order to reach the northern counties it decided to situate it in Derry, even though Derry is in fact not a part of the Republic of Ireland.

But just geographically, in order to reach that part of the Republic of Ireland and the counties in Northern Ireland that are part of the U.K. decided that that would geographically be the smartest place to put it as that's a big population center.

Now they are concerned what happens if you have different regulations regulating health and the research that goes into cancer, what that will do for pharmaceuticals. Essentially, it creates a massive headache.

With the breakdown of talks on Monday where one moment Financial Times is reporting breakthrough deal and the BBC reporting the same thing, and then about an hour later, not so fast.

This week has, obviously, been tumultuous—probably the most tumultuous on the border issue. Again, Dr. Wright, if you could discuss the various political issues at play.

I have had a number of colleagues come up to me asking me so what exactly is this about, and if you could elaborate on the issues that have prevented an agreed-upon solution to prevent a hard border, even though it seems to be something that Washington, London, Dublin, nationalists, and unionists all agree on and yet in practice difficult to achieve.

Mr. WRIGHT. Yes. Thank you.

The British Government, after Brexit, made it clear that Brexit meant leaving the single market and the customs union. So it would leave and the market that allowed for free movement of good, capital, services, and people and the common tariff area.

It is widely believed that if Britain leaves the customs union and the single market that there will have to be a customs border between Northern Ireland and the Republic of Ireland—that without it there would be too—there will be danger of smuggling. There will be all sorts of problems that would arise.

And so in order to prevent a hard border from happening, either the U.K. has to remain inside the single market and customs union as a whole or there needs to be what the diplomats I understand call—called regulatory alignment whereby Northern Ireland chooses to maintain the regulations of the single market and customs union so there would be no gap with the Republic of Ireland and there could be an open border.

And that position is unacceptable to the Democratic Unionist Party, which is providing support through a competence and supply agreement with Theresa May's government.

So they are unable to get that through without their support and as a result we are at a deadlock because the EU 27 including the Irish Government is very strongly of the view there is going to be a hard border. The DUP is opposed to the proposed solution.

The British Government also says it doesn't want a hard border. But it finds itself unable, I think, to support the solution that was identified.

Mr. BOYLE. Finally, I just want to ask about the special envoys. They are not specifically related to Brexit but, obviously, this is an area where a special envoy could help.

Could you speak a bit about the importance of the U.S. maintaining a special envoy, something that was supported by the Bush administration, obviously created under the Clinton administration.

That was the formal official role that George Mitchell had, something that has happened for the previous 20 years. And also, if you could address perhaps a perception by some in Washington who maybe aren't intimately involved in this issue who just assume oh, that's—that's all well and good, right?

Didn't they achieve peace and everyone lives happily ever after and maybe doesn't quite recognize them. Unfortunately, reality is not necessarily as rosy as that picture.

Mr. WRIGHT. Yes. Very briefly, you know, the U.S. has had a crucial role in the Northern Ireland peace process from the very beginning, and I think that's been critical to its success.

Secretary Tillerson abolished this position along with other special envoys. I think it made sense if this hadn't been happening because even though there are problems with the governance in Belfast. But with Brexit, I think it is particularly important to have U.S. engagement.

I would just raise one other issues as well that I didn't have in my written testimony. But I think there is also a role for a nongovernmental involvement by the former diplomats and political leaders who have been involved in Northern Ireland.

For instance, the Irish Government and EU, the U.K. could agree to set up an international commission led by an American that would try to identify solutions to the—to Brexit that uphold the Good Friday agreement.

They may be seen as more independently minded than the Irish Government is by the unionist community. So I think there are imaginative ways that we could proceed here.

But simply having no engagement whatsoever and treating it purely as an internal issue with no role for the United States I think is regrettable.

Mr. BOYLE. Yes, because, obviously, as we saw throughout the '70s and '80s, the British Government is not going to be perceived as a neutral arbiter by the nationalist community and the Irish Government in Dublin is not going to be perceived as a neutral arbiter by the unionist community, hence, the positive role that the U.S. can play, having a strong relationship with all sides.

Thank you very much.

Mr. ROHRABACHER. And yes, we are friends with both our British friends and our Irish friends, which makes us the perfect in between.

Let me just note there will always be a logical explanation of why we need to give all of our rights to make our own decisions away to some central government, maybe even some global government, and that led to some real problems even at the level that Great Britain had given up certain rights, as Mr. Gardiner had mentioned. The centralization and the bureaucracy that it spawned was not necessarily, or at least the British people obviously did not think it was in their interests.

Maybe you can tell us, Mr. Gardiner, what—your analysis of where the British people are at in all of this. Obviously, they voted by very recognizable majority that they wanted to separate from Brussels. What was their reason and tell us going from there.

Mr. GARDINER. Well, thank you very much for the question, and a very important question.

I think the reasons for Brexit are multiple. Primarily, the British people voted to leave the European Union to reestablish their own full sovereignty as a sovereign nation state, to take back control of British laws, Britain's borders, Britain's destiny as a free country, and I think the issue of self-determination was absolutely the heart of Brexit.

It was also, I think, a desire on the part of the British people to be able to really take full control of their own border, decide who comes into the country.

At the moment, Britain does not have that full control in terms of people coming in from the European Union.

But this was also, I think, a rejection of the European Union ruling elite seen as increasingly unaccountable, aloof, undemocratic.

It is not just in Britain I think that you have this momentum. You see it all over Europe in many European countries and the reality is that the European project today is viewed by I would say the majority of the British people as outdated.

It hasn't moved with the times. It is seen as a hugely centralized entity, a supranational entity that tramples upon the rights of individual nation states.

And so national sovereignty is fundamentally important to the British people and I believe that the U.S. Government actually fully understands that and I think the support given by the present U.S. administration for the British Government over Brexit has been very much welcomed by the British side and it is good that, you know, the White House supports Brexit and views Brexit as a powerful force that will strengthen the special relationship actually which indeed it will do.

But at the end of the day, Brexit was all about the desire on the part of the British people to once again be a truly free sovereign people. Those are universal extremely powerful principles.

Mr. ROHRABACHER. Excuse me. Is this same spirit not identified in several other areas in Europe where we have in Spain you have people who want to have their own government and you have various peoples now throughout the world actually that are suggesting that the right of self-determination is not something that just no longer exists in the souls of human beings in this modern age.

Let me just note that I believe that that same type of desire for a group of people to control their own destiny and not to be controlled by even a group of nations or a group of other people is just— it is part of what America was all about in the beginning and that— that spirit is still around in different parts of the world today.

And the more you have centralization I know that that's a different way of looking at government. The more centralized your government and distant is it, the more likely that those people holding power will be arrogant and less responsive than if you have someone in your local community or your state or even in your own country handling those same type of governmental decision making.

And could you, okay—could you please let us know what the trade is like between the United States and the EU versus the United States and just Great Britain?

Ms. CHORLINS. Certainly. The U.K., as I mentioned, is the U.S.'s fourth largest export destination and our seventh largest trading partner overall.

The EU is our single largest trading partner if you look at it as a unified market.

Mr. ROHRABACHER. Now, does that include Great Britain?

Ms. CHORLINS. Yes, it does.

Mr. ROHRABACHER. Okay. So how much—I am trying to see how much of that trade thing is Great Britain and the two entities as compared to one another?

Ms. CHORLINS. I don't have specific facts at my disposal but I am happy to provide that in my written answers to the subcommittee.

Mr. ROHRABACHER. I'd like to—please do, because when we are trying to figure out the economic, you know, impact of this, exactly whether or not the EU is in itself absent of Great Britain is—dominates or whether Great Britain is actually a major force in this. We need to know. Dr. Gardiner already has mentioned that the stock market in Great Britain is soaring. Is that correct?

Mr. GARDINER. Well, it has soared since the Brexit referendum and I'd say that, you know, Britain is doing extremely well in the Brexit era, including in terms of foreign direct investment, which has risen significantly over the past year and tens of thousands of new jobs have been created in the U.K. since the Brexit referendum.

It is significant that Google, actually, is building a brand new European headquarters in London at the cost of $1 billion, employing 7,000 people.

It is a sign of U.S. confidence in Great Britain and the United States has invested in the U.K. about $5 trillion worth of corporate assets. That's 22 percent of America's total overseas corporate assets invested.

Mr. ROHRABACHER. Now, I find that predictions of gloom and doom when someone is trying to make political determinations usually are absolutely wrong—I mean, just totally wrong.

And we had—don't want to rub it in too much but the fact is that we were going to face a major economic crisis and the stock market was going to the bottom if our current President was elected and it has had—and we have seen just the opposite.

And so when trying to determine what economic viability is we should actually look at the figures, figure out what is—and let me ask Dr. Wright.

So what do you predict in terms of economically this—a separate entity with Great Britain? Is this going to be a positive economic force for both Britain, maybe even Europe, or is this going to be a negative force?

Mr. WRIGHT. I think it is negative for both the U.K. and the EU Brexit, I think, will damage the U.K. in several respects.

The first is that the proposal by the British Government is to engage on this global economic diplomacy to secure trade deals with all sorts of countries including the U.S. They are doing so at a time when protectionist sentiment is at post-Cold War high. So it is extremely difficult to negotiate trade deals in that environment.

The city of London, which is probably Britain's most important services economy I think will lose much of its ability to do business for the EU because of the lack of what's called passporting rights that it enjoys under the single market.

Mr. ROHRABACHER. So you're predicting a, for——

Mr. WRIGHT. There will, I think, be something of a—something of a decline. The other—the other—I don't know how large it will be but I think it will—it will damage the British economy overall. And the final point is that it is often said that Britain can de- regulate if it leaves the single market and reduces the number of regulations.

The opposite is also possible. If Jeremy Corbyn were to be elected Prime Minister, he will be free to massively increase U.S. regulation beyond that which is enjoyed—which is imposed by the EU at the moment.

So you could easily see the arrow going the other direction as well. So I think it is quite risky. That being said, they have decided to leave, which is why I have argued for as close an economic relationship between the U.K. and the EU and between the U.S. and the U.K. and the EU.

So I think it is important to make sure that this works if this is what they want to do. But I don't think we should believe that there is enormous economic opportunities out there that have not been availed of to date.

Mr. ROHRABACHER. And Dr. Gardiner, you're not—you're pretty optimistic as compared to pessimistic?

Mr. GARDINER. Yes. Actually, I mean, just in response to Dr. Wright's comments, I would say that there is no evidence whatsoever of any flight of capital out of the city of London since the Brexit referendum. In fact, quite the opposite is happening.

And as we saw, when Britain decided not to be part of the European single currency, the city of London, the world's biggest financial center, thrived and prospered outside of the single currency and I think we are going to see the same thing with Britain outside of the—outside of the European Union, freed of the immense regulatory burdens that exist within the EU.

And so there is not a shred of evidence to suggest that Britain's economy or the city of London will suffer as a result of being outside of the European Union. Not one U.S. investment bank, for example, has decided to close its offices in London and relocate elsewhere in Europe.

So American confidence and global confidence in the U.K. is extremely high and already Britain is beginning to enter into trade discussions—negotiations with over 70 countries across the world.

And so there is every reason to believe there will be a highly successful U.S.-U.K. free trade deal and trade agreements between the United Kingdom, the world's fifth largest economy, and nations across the—across the globe.

Mr. ROHRABACHER. Well, thank you, and we will wait and see what happens and then we will—some—one of you guys are going to have to buy the round of drinks for whoever—whoever was right on this one.

Ms. CHORLINS. Mr. Chairman, I would just note that while it is the case that jobs may not yet have moved from American companies who are present in the U.K., it is very much the case that American companies have significant contingency plans in place and some of them have in fact announced their decision to move some part of their employee base from the U.K. to the continent because of this uncertainty about the relationship in the future. That's just the practical reality.

Mr. ROHRABACHER. So when—we will wait and see if Britain has a market that will attract more companies back. Then it is making its own decisions as compared to whether it is making its economic decisions with all those other countries being involved and setting the policy that Great Britain will have just like everybody else.

So with that said, Mr. Meeks.

Mr. MEEKS. Thank you, Mr. Chairman.

I was going to ask that very same question because I know in our—talking to some of our—coming from New York, my financial services community where we have got, you know, huge trade in financial service and in services that they are talking about contingency plans now as to whether they move.

Some, of course, coming back to New York and staying there but others are looking at some other European cities because they also want that connection with the EU because they are, you know, as you said, collectively part of our largest trading bloc collectively and they are trying to figure out how they will continue with both because they are significant—it is significant for both the EU and the U.K.

I am just—one of my concerns, of course, is I think that the unity of the EU and setting rules collectively together, working together, and we have been looking at standards even with the United States.

It helps us with global trade and the economies all of over the place. The lack of that is why I started out in my statement of lose-lose-lose.

I see there is opportunities for each and every one of us to lose in that regards if we don't figure out how to make sure that we are working on doing this thing collectively, which is why—and I'll start with you, Dr. Wright.

I didn't, you know, try to figure out why then would Prime Minister May commit to bringing the U.K. outside of the custom union and single market, thereby having a hard Brexit early in the negotiations since, certainly, it would make sense for Britain to remain within the customs union, I think, similarly like Turkey has, considering how much trade the U.K. and the EU. does.

So, I mean, can you give me any—fathom of the reasons why or difficulties that are——

Mr. WRIGHT. Yes, absolutely.

I think that the—it is a terrific question. I think the short answer is that to remain part of the single market, which would allow them to essentially continue to trade in the financial services sector and all of its other service industries, would have meant accepting the free movement of peoples because there are four freedoms to the single market—goods, services, capital, and people.

And the EU has said that those are indivisible. You cannot cherry pick and say we are going to take three of the four.

The U.K., I think, would like to cherry pick and would like to take some of those and keep their access on those but reject the others and the EU has rejected that because the integrity of the single market is of vital importance to them and as a result Theresa May's—Theresa May's government has said it is leaving the single markets and customs union.

I would be interested in Nile's view on that, too. I am not sure we'd probably disagree much on the diagnosis of why that's the case. But I think that's the nub of the—of the disagreement.

Mr. GARDINER. Yes, that's an excellent question.

So I think Dr. Wright has made some very good points. It would be really impossible for the United Kingdom to remain inside the customs union and the single market if it is to become a truly sovereign nation.

If Britain remains inside the customs union it would not be able to negotiate its own free trade agreements and this—this is a big part of Brexit, the idea of Britain being a truly global actor free to negotiate its own free trade deals all over the world including with the United States.

As a member of the—as a member of the customs union, Britain would not be able to that. As a member of the single market, Britain, as Dr. Wright mentioned, would not be able to control its borders.

It would have no say really over who comes in from the rest of Europe. And so fundamentally important issues.

And so the British view to retake control and reasserts its sovereignty. And so remaining in the single market and the customs union would be impossible if it was to honor those commitments.

Mr. MEEKS. It sounds to me that you're talking about part of the issue with Brexit has more—has also to do with migration and the problems that was taking place on the European continent as opposed to talking about, as Mrs. Chorlins is talking about, the integration of markets where we can do trade and collectively there is the free flow of business going across these borders. Is that not correct?

Mr. GARDINER. I think certainly that's—the issue of border control and immigration was an important factor in the Brexit—in the Brexit referendum—a major issue.

But I do believe that Britain is in a position to negotiate a strong free trade agreement with the European Union. Britain should continue to be able to have that access to European markets.

It is in the interest of the United Kingdom and the EU to reach an agreement that is good for both sides. After all, a huge amount of exports from the EU go into the U.K.

You look, for example, at the German car market. About one in every four or five German cars goes to Britain. And so it is Germany's interest to strike a good—a good deal.

And I think that a free trade agreement between both sides actually would be in the interest of both Britain and the—and the European Union.

Mr. MEEKS. Except I have found that, you know, sometimes initially it is thought that the EU would just accept whatever the U.K. said in this.

U.K. would be able to dominate that discussion and the U.K. I think is finding out now that the EU is not just going to give them whatever they want. That is not what the realities are starting to show, and as a result, there is going to be a give and take.

And I know in talking to some of our companies in the United States as a result because one of the things that business does not like—and I'll ask Mrs. Chorlins—is uncertainty where you don't know, because they have to plan for five and 10 and 15 years down the road.

They can't move, you know, just with—on whim with an uncertainty. So I think that would have—that's going to affect overall how we determine and where we negotiate free trade agreements. In fact, Mrs. Chorlins, you said that we will want to do some- thing with the U.K. when the time was right. That was an important piece—when the time is right. When would that be?

I mean, I understand from the agreement with the—with Brexit and that you can't negotiate anything until at least after 2 years after the deal is done.

So how far down the road is it and how does that affect the thinking of our American companies as to how they are going to do business or where they are going to do business, whether it is in the EU or the U.K. or anyplace else and try to do a deal.

Ms. CHORLINS. Mr. Ranking Member, I think you touched on a very important point about the need for certainty and that's why the business community has been as active in pursuing or following these negations.

As far as when the U.S. and U.K. could actually negotiate a trade agreement between themselves, that's driven largely by when the EU and U.K. complete their negotiations.

Until we know what the U.K.'s relationship will look like with the EU, it will be impossible really for us to know what the right terms should be for a U.K.-U.S. negotiation.

So the timing really is largely driven by the pace at which the U.K. and the EU negotiate their own future trade arrangement.

But you're absolutely right, certainty is something that the business community is eagerly looking for in this process, and we have gone out of our way to make clear to both the U.K. and the EU governments that uncertainty about the way forward is going to have a detrimental economic effect.

Mr. MEEKS. And then, you know, because it becomes important, you know, to me still once Brexit is done that the EU and the U.K. still have relationships.

But my question is how will the U.K. be able to maintain a friction-free trade with the EU's internal market after leaving it because it rules out the European court of justice jurisdiction and continued regulatory alignments.

So how is that going to work?

Ms. CHORLINS. Mr. Ranking Member, I think you've put your finger on what is the I don't know how many billion euro question. But the real issue is, indeed, how do you structure a relationship that minimizes the friction when you have to thrash out issues such as the Irish border where we risk serious delays if a border is reimposed and there is real economic cost associated with that. I think that we have yet to see from either the U.K. or the EU clear indications of what their thinking is about the future relationship between those two.

Clearly, both sides want to sustain a strong relationship. They need each other. But how that works in practical terms is very much an open question and one that both sides are working through in very real time.

Mr. MEEKS. Mr. Wright, do you want to add anything? Dr. Wright. Excuse me.

Mr. WRIGHT. Yes. There is no way, I think, for the U.K. to have as much access as it currently does if it leaves to single market and the customs union. It is just impossible.

Any deal that they do will be significantly less in terms of access. A deal will not be agreed by March 2019. By March 2019, they propose only to have a broad political statement about what the deal would look like.

It would then take many years for the trade deal to be negotiated. It has to be ratified by every single country in the EU including several by referendum.

So during that period of time there will be a transition deal under which it almost looks certain that Britain will have to abide by all of the rules of the single market and customs union without any influence or votes. And so there is a problem about how that deal would be structured.

I think that—I very much agree with you. I think that is why remaining in the customs union and the single market would be a better choice for the U.K.

But this government has decided not to do that. Interestingly, it was not necessarily a key part of the referendum campaign. Some people said that. Some people did not.

And so there wasn't a unified position on it in advance. But I think therein lies the risk for the U.S. economy because the U.S. really needs a strong U.K. and a strong EU. It was mentioned a number of times in this but the U.S. actually does benefit from the EU.

If there is a Eurozone crisis or a breakup of the Eurozone, that will cause a global financial crisis. The EU is a vital partner of the U.S. and economic security like sanctions that isn't a part of NATO or any other military organization.

You know, so it has all of these—it has all of these benefits for the U.S. So I think moving the lose-lose-lose to a win-win I think is a major challenge.

Mr. MEEKS. And the way we do things today when you're talking about trade I think Mrs. Chorlins talked about it—data flows, which is important and how that's worked, and supply chain.

You know, as we are talking about trade now, supply chain is important. This is the way it develops. We no longer, you know, the economy and trade we did it in the 19th and 20th century.

This is the 21st century. Globalization is here. Things go faster in speed than ever imagined before and there is interconnectedness that depends upon our strength and if there is a part of the chain that is weak then it could hurt and be devastating to everybody as we saw what took place when we had the financial crisis in the United States in 2008.

It affected everybody and not just the United States, and that's why this is so important to all of us, whether you come from— whether you're part of the EU or now a part of the U.K. and, of course, the United States and why I feel that we have got to make sure that there is, and we tell them this so that can be a win-win-win because if we don't, we all will be victimized and lose from it.

And I yield back to you.

Mr. ROHRABACHER. Well, thank you very much and thank you, Mr. Meeks. I think we have had a very worthwhile discussion. I am going to wait and see which one of you two guys in particular—she was right there in the middle of all the facts but you guys had your—have your opinions on this. This isn't a safe seat or this is so we will watch and see.

Let me just note that I am really proud that the United States led the way on this whole idea of self-determination. I think that our Declaration of Independence says it all. Government only derives its powers from the consent of the governed and people have a right and must declare their right to control their own destiny, and we declared that in our Declaration of Independence.

That spirit, I think, is alive today and not just in Great Britain but in other areas of the world where people are no longer accepting the domination of other groups of people. And I think that when you have a bureaucracy, and bureaucracies are always arrogant, even if they are local bureaucracies, but they become ever more arrogant and ineffective as far away from those people who they are regulating as they go.

The farther away they go, the more arrogant it is, and I think of the people I know in Great Britain who talked about Brussels had a deep-seated just antagonistic relationship with Brussels—people over there who they don't know who they are and maybe don't even like people in Britain are making decisions for them, economic decisions that affected their lives.

I think that whole spirit—I know there are a lot of people who think the spirit of nationalism is a negative force in this world. I think that those—the greatest sins that have been committed against the people on this planet, the human race, have been done so by some not nationalistic enterprise but instead by some global vision of whether it is radical Islamic global world or whether it is some sort of communist world—some ideal that they were going to superimpose and that all the different things would then disappear because you'd have a centralized government or based on benevolence and the benevolence of those people would just come out naturally. I don't think so. I don't think that's what government—I don't think that's what happens. I don't think that's what actually history will record, as the bigger the government gets and the further away and the more it is going to control our lives for the benefit of all, the more people get stepped on and the less progress there is.

This is especially true, I believe, in this modern age, and the fact is today smaller entities of government, whether it is Great Britain as compared to all of Europe or whether it is Singapore, whether it is—whatever entities are there, you can do now—you've got global communications and global transfers of wealth in one form or another in order to do business, and that didn't happen in the years before. Maybe you needed a bigger government at that time. But now you can have small entities that are communicating with big entities all over the world.

I'll be waiting to see whether or not, once this thing is—all these things are settled—whether or not more people will be trying to invest in Europe or whether more people will go to Great Britain that is a—that is now separated from the EU. That will be a very important historic occasion and it is ours to see what happens with this.

So thank you for leading our discussion today. Thank you, Gregory, for your major—he always contributes. It is always right to the matter. We disagree on some things. But he is really a genius and we love him.

So with that said, thank you all. This hearing is adjourned.

[Whereupon, at 3:56 p.m., the committee was adjourned.]

APPENDIX

______

MATERIAL SUBMITTED FOR THE RECORD

SUBCOMMITTEE HEARING NOTICE
COMMITTEE ON FOREIGN AFFAIRS
U.S. HOUSE OF REPRESENTATIVES
WASHINGTON, DC 20515-6128

Subcommittee on Europe, Eurasia, and Emerging Threats
Dana Rohrabacher (R-CA), Chairman

November 29, 2017

TO: MEMBERS OF THE COMMITTEE ON FOREIGN AFFAIRS

You are respectfully requested to attend an **OPEN** hearing of the Committee on Foreign Affairs to be held by the Subcommittee on Europe, Eurasia, and Emerging Threats in Room 2200 of the Rayburn House Office Building (and available live on the Committee website at http://www.ForeignAffairs.house.gov):

DATE: Wednesday, December 6, 2017

TIME: 2:00 p.m.

SUBJECT: Brexit: A Negotiation Update

WITNESSES: Nile Gardiner, Ph.D.
                    Director
                    Margaret Thatcher Center for Freedom
                    The Heritage Foundation

                    Ms. Marjorie Chorlins
                    Vice President for European Affairs, and
                    Executive Director of the U.S.-U.K. Business Council
                    U.S. Chamber of Commerce

                    Thomas Wright, Ph.D.
                    Director
                    Center on the United States and Europe
                    Brookings Institution

By Direction of the Chairman

COMMITTEE ON FOREIGN AFFAIRS

MINUTES OF SUBCOMMITTEE ON _________ *Europe, Eurasia, and Emerging Threats* _________ HEARING

Day __*Wednesday*__ Date __*December 6, 2017*__ Room __*2200 RHOB*__

Starting Time __*2:30 pm*__ Ending Time __*3:56 pm*__

Recesses __*0*__ (____to____)(____to____)(____to____)(____to____)(____to____)(____to____)

Presiding Member(s)
Rep. Rohrabacher

Check all of the following that apply:

Open Session ☑
Executive (closed) Session ☐
Televised ☐

Electronically Recorded (taped) ☑
Stenographic Record ☑

TITLE OF HEARING:

Brexit: A Neogtiation Update

SUBCOMMITTEE MEMBERS PRESENT:

Rep. Meeks, Rep. Curtis, Rep. Kelly

NON-SUBCOMMITTEE MEMBERS PRESENT: *(Mark with an * if they are not members of full committee.)*

Rep. Boyle

HEARING WITNESSES: Same as meeting notice attached? Yes ☑ **No** ☐
(If "no", please list below and include title, agency, department, or organization.)

STATEMENTS FOR THE RECORD: *(List any statements submitted for the record.)*

Attached

TIME SCHEDULED TO RECONVENE __________
or
TIME ADJOURNED __*3: 56 pm*__

____
Subcommittee Staff Associate

Questions for the Record
Rep. F. James Sensenbrenner, Jr.
Subcommittee on Europe, Eurasia, and Emerging Threats
"Brexit: A Negotiation Update"
December 6, 2017

For Mr. Gardiner:

1. The United Kingdom (UK) Territory of Gibraltar is one of America's strongest allies in the Mediterranean region. After the Brexit vote, the Spanish Foreign Minister expressed Spain's intention to use the vote to exert pressure on Gibraltar, related to Spain's ongoing challenge to Gibraltar's sovereignty as a UK territory. European Union (EU) officials have confirmed that once UK leaves the EU on March 29, 2019, Gibraltar will not enjoy the same protection with the transition period as the rest of the UK. This could cause Gibraltar to drop out of the single market and the customs union immediately. How concerned should the U.S. government be, post-Brexit, about the well-being of Gibraltar and its continued strength as a U.S. ally?
2. Throughout the course of the Brexit process, what can the U.S. government do to reaffirm our continuing alliance with Gibraltar and our longstanding strategic relationship with them?

[NOTE: Responses to these questions were not received prior to printing.]

Questions for the Record - Rep. Robin Kelly
EE&ET Subcommittee Hearing, *Brexit: A Negotiation Update*
December 6, 2017

1. How do you predict the issue of land borders will end with Ireland and Spain? What U.S. interests are at stake should there be a hard Brexit?

2. Following Brexit, the UK will have to rapidly reach trade deals with dozens of countries following the EU. How do you expect the United Kingdom to make themselves more attractive to businesses if they no longer offer a gateway to the European Union market? What are possible hurdles to US-UK trade deals?

[NOTE: Responses to these questions were not received prior to printing.]